MW00474723

SPIRIT

of

FAITH

the
ONENESS
of RELIGION

SPIRIT
of
FAITH

the
ONENESS
of RELIGION

compiled by Bahá'í Publishing

Bahá'í
PUBLISHING

Wilmette, Illinois

Bahá'í Publishing
415 Linden Avenue, Wilmette, Illinois 60091-2844
Copyright © 2011 by the National Spiritual Assembly
of the Bahá'ís of the United States

All rights reserved. Published 2011
Printed in the United States of America on acid-free
paper ∞

14   13   12   11   4   3   2   1

Library of Congress Cataloging-in-Publication Data
Spirit of faith : the oneness of religion / compiled by
Baha'i Publishing.
     p. cm.
  Includes bibliographical references and index.
  ISBN 978-1-931847-81-0 (alk. paper)
  1. Bahai Faith—Doctrines. 2. Religion—Philosophy.
I. Bahá'u'lláh, 1817–1892. Selections. English. II. Bab,
'Ali Muhammad Shirazi, 1819–1850. Selections. English.
III. 'Abdu'l-Bahá, 1844–1921. Selections. English. IV.
Baha'i Publishing.
  BP360.S6913 2011
  297.9'32—dc22

                                        2011000231

Cover design by Andrew Johnson
Book design by Patrick Falso

CONTENTS

INTRODUCTION

The Oneness of Religion is the second book in Bahá'í Publishing's *Spirit of Faith* series, which explores weighty spiritual topics—such as the oneness of God, the oneness of humankind, the promise of world peace, and much more—by taking an in-depth look at how the Bahá'í writings view these issues. Bahá'í Publishing hopes that this series will continue to help bring the fundamental beliefs of the Bahá'í Faith to the receptive reader.

Bahá'ís believe in the essential unity of God, and the passages in this compilation reveal that all religions share their source from one same God, Who has progressively revealed teachings to humanity over time. We may have different names or traditions to praise Him, but ultimately God is one, and we are all part of His creation. The differences and conflicts in our world today are not the result of God's teachings; rather, they are the product of a humanity that has strayed far from its Creator and is need of spiritual renewal. Included in this compilation are passages from the writings of Bahá'u'lláh, the Prophet and Founder of the Bahá'í Faith, Whose name means "the Glory of God"; those of His forerunner, the Báb; and the writings and recorded utterances of Bahá'u'lláh's eldest son and successor, 'Abdu'l-Bahá.

The Bahá'í Faith is an independent world religion that began in 1844 in Persia (present-day Iran). Since its inception, the Bahá'í Faith has spread to 235 nations and territories and has been accepted by more than five million people. Bahá'ís believe that there is only one God, that all the major world religions come from God, and that all the members of the human race are essentially members of one family. Bahá'ís strive to eliminate all forms of prejudice and believe that people of all races, nations, social status, and religious backgrounds are equal in the sight of God. The Bahá'í Faith also teaches that each individual is responsible for the independent investigation of truth, that science and religion are in harmony, and that men and women are equal in the sight of God.

It is hoped that this compilation helps demonstrate the essential unity of the world's religions—a unity that can lead to a greater sense of understanding between people of all faiths, and ultimately to a brighter future for humanity.

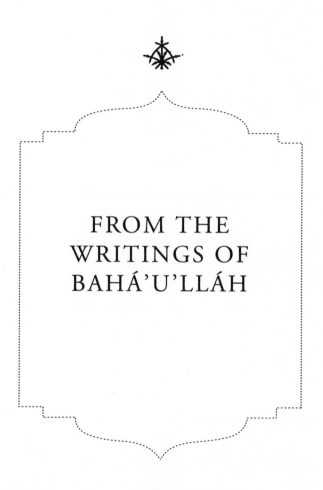

FROM THE
WRITINGS OF
BAHÁ'U'LLÁH

1

The Divine Messengers have been sent down, and their Books were revealed, for the purpose of promoting the knowledge of God, and of furthering unity and fellowship amongst men.

2

Every true Prophet hath regarded His Message as fundamentally the same as the Revelation of every other Prophet gone before Him.

3

Every Prophet Whom the Almighty and Peerless Creator hath purposed to send to the peoples of the earth hath been entrusted with a Message, and charged to act in a manner that would best meet the requirements of the age in which He appeared.

4

The purpose underlying the revelation of every heavenly Book, nay, of every divinely revealed verse, is to endue all men with righteousness and understanding, so that peace and tranquility may be firmly established amongst them. Whatsoever instilleth assurance into the hearts of men, whatsoever exalteth their station or promoteth their contentment, is acceptable in the sight of God.

5

Religion is verily the chief instrument for the establishment of order in the world and of tranquility amongst its peoples.

6

From the foregoing passages and allusions it hath been made indubitably clear that in the kingdoms of earth and heaven there must needs be manifested a Being, an Essence Who shall act as a Manifestation and Vehicle for the transmission of the grace of the Divinity Itself, the Sovereign Lord of all. Through the Teachings of this Daystar of Truth every man will advance and develop until he attaineth the station at which he can manifest all the potential forces with which his inmost true self hath been endowed. It is for this very purpose that in every age and dispensation the Prophets of God and His chosen Ones have appeared amongst men, and have evinced such power as is born of God and such might as only the Eternal can reveal.

7

I testify before God that each one of these Manifestations hath been sent down through the operation of the Divine Will and Purpose, that each hath been the bearer of a specific Message, that each hath been entrusted with a divinely revealed Book and been commissioned to unravel the mysteries of a mighty Tablet.

8

It is clear and evident to thee that all the Prophets are the Temples of the Cause of God, Who have appeared clothed in divers attire. If thou wilt observe with discriminating eyes, thou wilt behold Them all abiding in the same tabernacle, soaring in the same heaven, seated upon the same throne, uttering the same speech, and proclaiming the same Faith. Such is the unity of those Essences of Being, those Luminaries of infinite and immeasurable splendor!

9

He hath in every age and cycle, in conformity with His transcendent wisdom, sent forth a divine Messenger to revive the dispirited and despondent souls with the living waters of His utterance, One Who is indeed the Expounder, the true Interpreter, inasmuch as man is unable to comprehend that which hath streamed forth from the Pen of Glory and is recorded in His heavenly Books. Men at all times and under all conditions stand in need of one to exhort them, guide them and to instruct and teach them. Therefore He hath sent forth His Messengers, His Prophets and chosen ones that they might acquaint the people with the divine purpose underlying the revelation of Books and the raising up of Messengers, and that everyone may become aware of the trust of God which is latent in the reality of every soul.

10

In truth, religion is a radiant light and an impregnable stronghold for the protection and welfare of the peoples of the world, for the fear of God impelleth man to hold fast to that which is good, and shun all evil. Should the lamp of religion be obscured, chaos and confusion will ensue, and the lights of fairness and justice, of tranquility and peace cease to shine. Unto this will bear witness every man of true understanding.

11

The purpose of religion as revealed from the heaven of God's holy Will is to establish unity and concord amongst the peoples of the world; make it not the cause of dissension and strife. The religion of God and His divine law are the most potent instruments and the surest of all means for the dawning of the light of unity amongst men. The progress of the world, the development of nations, the tranquility of peoples, and the peace of all who dwell on earth are among the principles and ordinances of God. Religion bestoweth upon man the most precious of all gifts, offereth the cup of prosperity, imparteth eternal life, and showereth imperishable benefits upon mankind.

12

Know thou assuredly that the essence of all the Prophets of God is one and the same. Their unity is absolute. God, the Creator, saith: There is no distinction whatsoever among the Bearers of My Message. They all have but one purpose; their secret is the same secret. To prefer one in honor to another, to exalt certain ones above the rest, is in no wise to be permitted.

13

The fundamental purpose animating the Faith of God and His Religion is to safeguard the interests and promote the unity of the human race, and to foster the spirit of love and fellowship amongst men.

14

The essence of belief in Divine unity consisteth in regarding Him Who is the Manifestation of God and Him Who is the invisible, the inaccessible, the unknowable Essence as one and the same. By this is meant that whatever pertaineth to the former, all His acts and doings, whatever He ordaineth or forbiddeth, should be considered, in all their aspects, and under all circumstances, and without any reservation, as identical with the Will of God Himself. This is the loftiest station to which a true believer in the unity of God can ever hope to attain. Blessed is the man that reacheth this station, and is of them that are steadfast in their belief.

15

The Purpose of the one true God, exalted be His glory, in revealing Himself unto men is to lay bare those gems that lie hidden within the mine of their true and inmost selves. That the divers communions of the earth, and the manifold systems of religious belief, should never be allowed to foster the feelings of animosity among men, is, in this Day, of the essence of the Faith of God and His Religion. These principles and laws, these firmly established and mighty systems, have proceeded from one Source, and are the rays of one Light. That they differ one from another is to be attributed to the varying requirements of the ages in which they were promulgated.

16

Beware, O believers in the Unity of God, lest ye be tempted to make any distinction between any of the Manifestations of His Cause, or to discriminate against the signs that have accompanied and proclaimed their Revelation. This indeed is the true meaning of Divine Unity, if ye be of them that apprehend and believe this truth. Be ye assured, moreover, that the works and acts of each and every one of these Manifestations of God, nay whatever pertaineth unto them, and whatsoever they may manifest in the future, are all ordained by God, and are a reflection of His Will and Purpose. Whoso maketh the slightest possible difference between their persons, their words, their messages, their acts and manners, hath indeed disbelieved in God, hath repudiated His signs, and betrayed the Cause of His Messengers.

17

He is really a believer in the Unity of God who recognizeth in each and every created thing the sign of the revelation of Him Who is the Eternal Truth, and not he who maintaineth that the creature is indistinguishable from the Creator.

18

The Pen of the Most High hath, at all times and under all conditions, remembered, with joy and tenderness, His loved ones, and hath counseled them to follow in His way. Well is it with him whom the changes and chances of this world have failed to deter from recognizing the Dayspring of the Unity of God, who hath quaffed, with unswerving resolve, and in the name of the Self-Subsisting, the sealed wine of His Revelation. Such a man shall be numbered with the inmates of Paradise, in the Book of God, the Lord of all worlds.

19

It is evident to thee that the Bearers of the trust of God are made manifest unto the peoples of the earth as the Exponents of a new Cause and the Bearers of a new Message. Inasmuch as these Birds of the Celestial Throne are all sent down from the heaven of the Will of God, and as they all arise to proclaim His irresistible Faith, they therefore are regarded as one soul and the same person. For they all drink from the one Cup of the love of God, and all partake of the fruit of the same Tree of Oneness.

20

There can be no doubt whatever that the peoples of the world, of whatever race or religion, derive their inspiration from one heavenly Source, and are the subjects of one God. The difference between the ordinances under which they abide should be attributed to the varying requirements and exigencies of the age in which they were revealed. All of them, except a few which are the outcome of human perversity, were ordained of God, and are a reflection of His Will and Purpose. Arise and, armed with the power of faith, shatter to pieces the gods of your vain imaginings, the sowers of dissension amongst you. Cleave unto that which draweth you together and uniteth you. This, verily, is the most exalted Word which the Mother

Book hath sent down and revealed unto you. To this beareth witness the Tongue of Grandeur from His habitation of glory.

21

Consider . . . the revelation of the light of the Name of God, the Incomparable. Behold, how this light hath enveloped the entire creation, how each and every thing manifesteth the sign of His Unity, testifieth to the reality of Him Who is the Eternal Truth, proclaimeth His sovereignty, His oneness, and His power.

22

That which God hath ordained as the sovereign remedy and mightiest instrument for the healing of the world is the union of all its peoples in one universal Cause, one common Faith.

23

Immerse yourselves in the ocean of My words, that ye may unravel its secrets, and discover all the pearls of wisdom that lie hid in its depths. Take heed that ye do not vacillate in your determination to embrace the truth of this Cause—a Cause through which the potentialities of the might of God have been revealed, and His sovereignty established. With faces beaming with joy, hasten ye unto Him. This is the changeless Faith of God, eternal in the past, eternal in the future. Let him that seeketh, attain it; and as to him that hath refused to seek it—verily, God is Self-Sufficient, above any need of His creatures.

24

As the body of man needeth a garment to clothe it, so the body of mankind must needs be adorned with the mantle of justice and wisdom. Its robe is the Revelation vouchsafed unto it by God. Whenever this robe hath fulfilled its purpose, the Almighty will assuredly renew it. For every age requireth a fresh measure of the light of God. Every Divine Revelation hath been sent down in a manner that befitted the circumstances of the age in which it hath appeared.

25

We have erewhile declared—and Our Word is the truth—: "Consort with the followers of all religions in a spirit of friendliness and fellowship."

26

I testify that by Thy Name the heaven of under-standing hath been adorned, and the ocean of utterance hath surged, and the dispensations of Thy providence have been promulgated unto the followers of all religions.

27

O followers of all religions! We behold you wandering distraught in the wilderness of error. Ye are the fish of this Ocean; wherefore do ye withhold yourselves from that which sustaineth you? Lo, it surgeth before your faces. Hasten unto it from every clime. This is the day whereon the Rock [Peter] crieth out and shouteth, and celebrateth the praise of its Lord, the All-Possessing, the Most High, saying: "Lo! The Father is come, and that which ye were promised in the Kingdom is fulfilled!" This is the Word which was preserved behind the veils of grandeur, and which, when the Promise came to pass, shed its radiance from the horizon of the Divine Will with clear tokens.

28

Religion bestoweth upon man the most precious of all gifts, offereth the cup of prosperity, imparteth eternal life, and showereth imperishable benefits upon mankind.

29

The second Ṭaráz is to consort with the followers of all religions in a spirit of friendliness and fellowship, to proclaim that which the Speaker on Sinai hath set forth and to observe fairness in all matters. They that are endued with sincerity and faithfulness should associate with all the peoples and kindreds of the earth with joy and radiance, inasmuch as consorting with people hath promoted and will continue to promote unity and concord, which in turn are conducive to the maintenance of order in the world and to the regeneration of nations. Blessed are such as hold fast to the cord of kindliness and tender mercy and are free from animosity and hatred.

30

If any man were to meditate on that which the Scriptures, sent down from the heaven of God's holy Will, have revealed, he would readily recognize that their purpose is that all men shall be regarded as one soul, so that the seal bearing the words "The Kingdom shall be God's" may be stamped on every heart, and the light of Divine bounty, of grace, and mercy may envelop all mankind.

31

Take fast hold of justice and adhere unto equity that perchance thou mayest not, for selfish motives, use religion as a snare, nor disregard the truth for the sake of gold.

32

The unbelievers and the faithless have set their minds on four things: first, the shedding of blood; second, the burning of books; third, the shunning of the followers of other religions; fourth, the extermination of other communities and groups. Now however, through the strengthening grace and potency of the Word of God these four barriers have been demolished, these clear injunctions have been obliterated from the Tablet and brutal dispositions have been transmuted into spiritual attributes.

33

S uch is the unity of those Essences of Being, those Luminaries of infinite and immeasurable splendor! Wherefore, should one of these Manifestations of Holiness proclaim saying: "I am the return of all the Prophets," He, verily, speaketh the truth. In like manner, in every subsequent Revelation, the return of the former Revelation is a fact, the truth of which is firmly established.

34

The purpose of God in creating man hath been, and will ever be, to enable him to know his Creator and to attain His Presence. To this most excellent aim, this supreme objective, all the heavenly Books and the divinely revealed and weighty Scriptures unequivocally bear witness. Whoso hath recognized the Dayspring of Divine guidance and entered His holy court hath drawn nigh unto God and attained His Presence, a Presence which is the real Paradise, and of which the loftiest mansions of heaven are but a symbol.

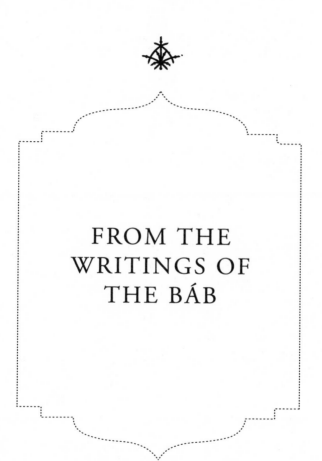

FROM THE
WRITINGS OF
THE BÁB

1

The Revelation of God may be likened to the sun. No matter how innumerable its risings, there is but one sun, and upon it depends the life of all things.

2

This Religion is indeed, in the sight of God, the essence of the Faith of Muḥammad; haste ye then to attain the celestial Paradise and the all-highest Garden of His good-pleasure in the presence of the One True God, could ye but be patient and thankful before the evidences of the signs of God.

3

The revelation of the Divine Reality hath everlastingly been identical with its concealment and its concealment identical with its revelation. That which is intended by "Revelation of God" is the Tree of divine Truth that betokeneth none but Him, and it is this divine Tree that hath raised and will raise up Messengers, and hath revealed and will ever reveal Scriptures. From eternity unto eternity this Tree of divine Truth hath served and will ever serve as the throne of the revelation and concealment of God among His creatures, and in every age is made manifest through whomsoever He pleaseth.

4

The One true God may be compared unto the sun and the believer unto a mirror. No sooner is the mirror placed before the sun than it reflects its light.

5

Since thou hast faithfully obeyed the true religion of God in the past, it behooveth thee to follow His true religion hereafter, inasmuch as every religion proceedeth from God, the Help in Peril, the Self-Subsisting.

6

Seek not proofs and evidences after thine idle fancy; but rather base thy proofs upon what God hath appointed. Moreover, know thou that neither being a man of learning nor being a follower is in itself a source of glory. If thou art a man of learning, thy knowledge becometh an honor, and if thou art a follower, thine adherence unto leadership becometh an honor, only when these conform to the good-pleasure of God. And beware lest thou regard as an idle fancy the good-pleasure of God; it is the same as the good-pleasure of His Messenger.

7

Become as true brethren in the one and indivisible religion of God, free from distinction, for verily God desireth that your hearts should become mirrors unto your brethren in the Faith, so that ye find yourselves reflected in them, and they in you. This is the true Path of God, the Almighty, and He is indeed watchful over your actions.

8

True knowledge, therefore, is the knowledge of God, and this is none other than the recognition of His Manifestation in each Dispensation. Nor is there any wealth save in poverty in all save God and sanctity from aught else but Him—a state that can be realized only when demonstrated towards Him Who is the Dayspring of His Revelation. This doth not mean, however, that one ought not to yield praise unto former Revelations. On no account is this acceptable, inasmuch as it behooveth man, upon reaching the age of nineteen, to render thanksgiving for the day of his conception as an embryo. For had the embryo not existed, how could he have reached his present state? Likewise had the religion taught by Adam not existed, this Faith would not have attained its present stage. Thus consider thou the development of God's Faith until the end that hath no end.

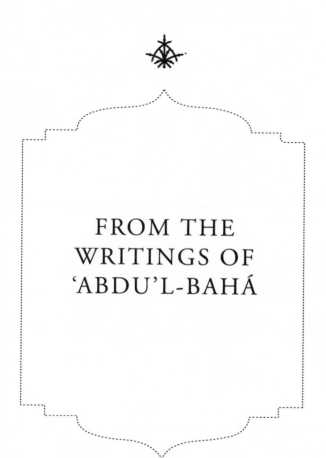

FROM THE
WRITINGS OF
'ABDU'L-BAHÁ

1

The essence of all religions is the Love of God, and it is the foundation of all the sacred teachings.

2

Religion is a mighty bulwark. If the edifice of religion shakes and totters, commotion and chaos will ensue and the order of things will be utterly upset, for in the world of mankind there are two safeguards that protect man from wrongdoing. One is the law which punishes the criminal; but the law prevents only the manifest crime and not the concealed sin; whereas the ideal safeguard, namely, the religion of God, prevents both the manifest and the concealed crime, trains man, educates morals, compels the adoption of virtues and is the all-inclusive power which guarantees the felicity of the world of mankind. But by religion is meant that which is ascertained by investigation and not that which is based on mere imitation, the foundations of Divine Religions and not human imitations.

3

It is the outward practices of religion that are so different, and it is they that cause disputes and enmity—while the reality is always the same, and one. The Reality is the Truth, and truth has no division. Truth is God's guidance, it is the light of the world, it is love, it is mercy. These attributes of truth are also human virtues inspired by the Holy Spirit.

4

The Reality of the divine Religions is one, because the Reality is one and cannot be two. All the prophets are united in their message, and unshaken. They are like the sun; in different seasons they ascend from different rising points on the horizon. Therefore every ancient prophet gave the glad tidings of the future, and every future has accepted the past.

5

The true foundation of all faiths must be established, the outer differences abolished. There must be a Oneness of Faith.

6

Religion . . . is not a series of beliefs, a set of customs; religion is the teachings of the Lord God, teachings which constitute the very life of humankind, which urge high thoughts upon the mind, refine the character, and lay the groundwork for man's everlasting honor.

7

The gift of God to this enlightened age is the knowledge of the oneness of mankind and of the fundamental oneness of religion.

8

The divine religions are like the progression of the seasons of the year. When the earth becomes dead and desolate and because of frost and cold no trace of vanished spring remains, the springtime dawns again and clothes everything with a new garment of life. The meadows become fresh and green, the trees are adorned with verdure and fruits appear upon them. Then the winter comes again, and all the traces of spring disappear. This is the continuous cycle of the seasons—spring, winter, then the return of spring. But though the calendar changes and the years move forward, each springtime that comes is the return of the springtime that has gone; this spring is the renewal of the former spring. Springtime is springtime, no matter when or how often it comes. The divine Prophets are as the coming of spring, each renewing and quickening the teachings of the Prophet Who came before Him.

9

Therefore, it is evident that God has destined and intended religion to be the cause and means of cooperative effort and accomplishment among mankind. To this end He has sent the Prophets of God, the holy Manifestations of the Word, in order that the fundamental reality and religion of God may prove to be the bond of human unity, for the divine religions revealed by these holy Messengers have one and the same foundation. All will admit, therefore, that the divine religions are intended to be the means of true human cooperation, that they are united in the purpose of making humanity one family, for they rest upon the universal foundation of love, and love is the first effulgence of Divinity.

From the Writings of 'Abdu'l-Bahá

10

The divine Manifestations since the day of Adam have striven to unite humanity so that all may be accounted as one soul. The function and purpose of a shepherd is to gather and not disperse his flock. The Prophets of God have been divine Shepherds of humanity. They have established a bond of love and unity among mankind, made scattered peoples one nation and wandering tribes a mighty kingdom. They have laid the foundation of the oneness of God and summoned all to universal peace. All these holy, divine Manifestations are one. They have served one God, promulgated the same truth, founded the same institutions and reflected the same light. Their appearances have been successive and correlated; each One has announced and extolled the One Who was to follow, and all laid the foundation of reality. They summoned and invited the people to love and made the human world a mirror of the Word of God. Therefore, the divine religions They established have one foundation; Their teachings, proofs and evidences are one; in name and form They differ, but in reality They agree and are the same.

11

The Lord of mankind has caused His holy, divine Manifestations to come into the world. He has revealed His heavenly Books in order to establish spiritual brotherhood and through the power of the Holy Spirit has made it practicable for perfect fraternity to be realized among mankind. And when through the breaths of the Holy Spirit this perfect fraternity and agreement are established amongst men—this brotherhood and love being spiritual in character, this loving-kindness being heavenly, these constraining bonds being divine—a unity appears which is indissoluble, unchanging and never subject to transformation.

12

Each of the holy Manifestations announced the glad tidings of His successor, and each One confirmed the message of His predecessor. Therefore, inasmuch as They were agreed and united in purpose and teaching, it is incumbent upon Their followers to be likewise unified in love and spiritual fellowship. In no other way will discord and alienation disappear and the oneness of the world of humanity be established.

13

From time immemorial the divine teachings have been successively revealed, and the bounties of the Holy Spirit have ever been emanating. All the teachings are one reality, for reality is single and does not admit multiplicity. Therefore, the divine Prophets are one, inasmuch as They reveal the one reality, the Word of God.

14

The Sun of Divinity and of Reality has revealed itself in various mirrors. Though these mirrors are many, yet the Sun is one. The bestowals of God are one; the reality of the divine religion is one. Consider how one and the same light has reflected itself in the different mirrors or manifestations of it.

15

The divine Manifestations have been iconoclastic in Their teachings, uprooting error, destroying false religious beliefs and summoning mankind anew to the fundamental oneness of God. All of Them have, likewise, proclaimed the oneness of the world of humanity.

16

The holy Manifestations Who have been the Sources or Founders of the various religious systems were united and agreed in purpose and teaching. Abraham, Moses, Zoroaster, Buddha, Jesus, Muḥammad, the Báb and Bahá'u'lláh are one in spirit and reality. Moreover, each Prophet fulfilled the promise of the One Who came before Him and, likewise, Each announced the One Who would follow.

17

Quench ye the fires of war, lift high the banners of peace, work for the oneness of humankind and remember that religion is the channel of love unto all peoples.

18

Truth is one in all religions, and by means of it the unity of the world can be realized.

19

The holy Manifestations of God, the divine Prophets, are the first Teachers of the human race. They are universal Educators, and the fundamental principles they have laid down are the causes and factors of the advancement of nations.

20

Unity is the essential truth of religion and, when so understood, embraces all the virtues of the human world. Praise be to God! This knowledge has been spread, eyes have been opened, and ears have become attentive. Therefore, we must endeavor to promulgate and practice the religion of God which has been founded by all the Prophets. And the religion of God is absolute love and unity.

21

The divine religions were founded for the purpose of unifying humanity and establishing universal peace. Any movement which brings about peace and agreement in human society is truly a divine movement; any reform which causes people to come together under the shelter of the same tabernacle is surely animated by heavenly motives.

22

It is evident that the fundamentals of religion are intended to unify and bind together; their purpose is universal, everlasting peace. Prior to the time of Jesus Christ the Word of God had unified opposite types and conflicting elements of human society; and since His appearance the divine Teachers of the primal principles of the law of God have all intended this universal outcome.

23

All humankind are as children in a school, and the Dawning-Points of Light, the Sources of divine revelation, are the teachers, wondrous and without peer. In the school of realities they educate these sons and daughters, according to teachings from God, and foster them in the bosom of grace, so that they may develop along every line, show forth the excellent gifts and blessings of the Lord, and combine human perfections; that they may advance in all aspects of human endeavor, whether outward or inward, hidden or visible, material or spiritual, until they make of this mortal world a widespread mirror, to reflect that other world which dieth not.

24

Each of the divine religions embodies two kinds of ordinances. The first is those which concern spiritual susceptibilities, the development of moral principles and the quickening of the conscience of man. These are essential or fundamental, one and the same in all religions, changeless and eternal— reality not subject to transformation. Abraham heralded this reality, Moses promulgated it, and Jesus Christ established it in the world of mankind. All the divine Prophets and Messengers were the instruments and channels of this same eternal, essential truth.

25

The divine religions must be the cause of oneness among men, and the means of unity and love; they must promulgate universal peace, free man from every prejudice, bestow joy and gladness, exercise kindness to all men and do away with every difference and distinction.

26

The unity which is productive of unlimited results is first a unity of mankind which recognizes that all are sheltered beneath the overshadowing glory of the All-Glorious, that all are servants of one God; for all breathe the same atmosphere, live upon the same earth, move beneath the same heavens, receive effulgence from the same sun and are under the protection of one God.

27

The foundations of the divine religions are one. If we investigate these foundations, we discover much ground for agreement, but if we consider the imitations of forms and ancestral beliefs, we find points of disagreement and division; for these imitations differ, while the sources and foundations are one and the same.

28

All the teaching of the Prophets is one; one faith; one Divine light shining throughout the world. Now, under the banner of the oneness of humanity all people of all creeds should turn away from prejudice and become friends and believers in all the Prophets. As Christians believe in Moses, so the Jews should believe in Jesus. As the Muḥammadans believe in Christ and Moses, so likewise the Jews and the Christians should believe in Muḥammad. Then all disputes would disappear, all then would be united. Bahá'u'lláh came for this purpose.

29

From the days of Adam until today, the religions of God have been made manifest, one following the other, and each one of them fulfilled its due function, revived mankind, and provided education and enlightenment. They freed the people from the darkness of the world of nature and ushered them into the brightness of the Kingdom. As each succeeding Faith and Law became revealed it remained for some centuries a richly fruitful tree and to it was committed the happiness of humankind.

30

The essential ordinances of religion were the same during the time of Abraham, the day of Moses and the cycle of Jesus, but the accidental or material laws were abrogated and superseded according to the exigency and requirement of each succeeding age. For example, in the law of Moses there were ten distinct commandments in regard to murder, which were revealed according to the requirement and capacity of the people, but in the day of Jesus these were abrogated and superseded in conformity with the changed and advanced human conditions.

31

The people of Islám were taught to realize how Jesus came from God and was born of the Spirit, and that He must be glorified of all men. Moses was a prophet of God, and revealed in His day and for the people to whom He was sent, the Book of God. Muḥammad recognized the sublime grandeur of Christ and the greatness of Moses and the prophets. If only the whole world would acknowledge the greatness of Muḥammad and all the Heaven-sent Teachers, strife and discord would soon vanish from the face of the earth, and God's Kingdom would come among men.

32

Our meaning is this: the religion of God is one, and it is the educator of humankind, but still, it needs must be made new. When thou dost plant a tree, its height increaseth day by day. It putteth forth blossoms and leaves and luscious fruits. But after a long time, it doth grow old, yielding no fruitage any more. Then doth the Husbandman of Truth take up the seed from that same tree, and plant it in a pure soil; and lo, there standeth the first tree, even as it was before.

33

Love ye all religions and all races with a love that is true and sincere and show that love through deeds and not through the tongue; for the latter hath no importance, as the majority of men are, in speech, well-wishers, while action is the best.

34

The essential basis of all the Divine Religions which pertains to the virtues of the world of mankind and is the foundation of the welfare of the world of man.

35

The essentials of the divine religion are one reality, indivisible and not multiple. It is one.

36

The clouds and mists of imitations have obscured the Sun of Truth. We must forsake these imitations, dispel these clouds and mists and free the Sun from the darkness of superstition. Then will the Sun of Truth shine most gloriously; then all the inhabitants of the world will be united, the religions will be one, sects and denominations will reconcile, all nationalities will flow together in the recognition of one Fatherhood, and all degrees of humankind will gather in the shelter of the same tabernacle, under the same banner.

37

The central purpose of the divine religions is the establishment of peace and unity among mankind. Their reality is one; therefore, their accomplishment is one and universal—whether it be through the essential or material ordinances of God. There is but one light of the material sun, one ocean, one rain, one atmosphere. Similarly, in the spiritual world there is one divine reality forming the center and altruistic basis for peace and reconciliation among various and conflicting nations and peoples.

38

Inasmuch as the essential reality of the religions is one and their seeming variance and plurality is adherence to forms and imitations which have arisen, it is evident that these causes of difference and divergence must be abandoned in order that the underlying reality may unite mankind in its enlightenment and upbuilding.

39

The underlying foundation of the religions is one; there is no intrinsic difference between them. Therefore, if the essential and fundamental ordinances of the religions be observed, peace and unity will dawn, and all the differences of sects and denominations will disappear.

40

O Thou kind Lord! Unite all. Let the religions agree and make the nations one, so that they may see each other as one family and the whole earth as one home. May they all live together in perfect harmony.

41

All the nations of the world will then be closely related and companionable, and the religions will merge into one, for the divine reality within them all is one reality.   •

42

Divine religion is not a cause for discord and disagreement. If religion becomes the source of antagonism and strife, the absence of religion is to be preferred. Religion is meant to be the quickening life of the body politic; if it be the cause of death to humanity, its nonexistence would be a blessing and benefit to man. Therefore, in this day the divine teachings must be sought, for they are the remedies for the present conditions of the world of humanity. The purpose of a remedy is to heal and cure.

43

These foundations of the Religion of God, which are spiritual and which are the virtues of humanity, cannot be abrogated; they are irremovable and eternal, and are renewed in the cycle of every Prophet.

44

The foundations of all the divine religions are peace and agreement, but misunderstandings and ignorance have developed. If these are caused to disappear, you will see that all the religious agencies will work for peace and promulgate the oneness of humankind. For the foundation of all is reality, and reality is not multiple or divisible. Moses founded it, Jesus raised its tent, and its brilliant light has shone forth in all the religions. Bahá'u'lláh proclaimed this one reality and spread the message of the Most Great Peace. Even in prison He rested not until He lighted this lamp in the East.

45

Religions are many, but the reality of religion is one. The days are many, but the sun is one. The fountains are many, but the fountainhead is one. The branches are many, but the tree is one.

46

Therefore, if the religions investigate reality and seek the essential truth of their own foundations, they will agree and no difference will be found. . . . These imitations may be likened to clouds which obscure the sunrise; but reality is the sun. If the clouds disperse, the Sun of Reality shines upon all, and no difference of vision will exist. The religions will then agree, for fundamentally they are the same. The subject is one, but predicates are many.

47

Bahá'u'lláh taught the Oneness of humanity; that is to say, all the children of men are under the mercy of the Great God. They are the sons of one God; they are trained by God. He has placed the crown of humanity on the head of every one of the servants of God. Therefore all nations and peoples must consider themselves brethren. They are all descendants from Adam. They are the branches, leaves, flowers and fruits of One Tree. They are pearls from one shell. But the children of men are in need of education and civilization, and they require to be polished, till they become bright and shining.

48

Nothing can be effected in the world, not even conceivably, without unity and agreement, and the perfect means for engendering fellowship and union is true religion.

49

The purpose . . . is to establish the fact that the religions of God are the true source of the spiritual and material perfections of man, and the fountainhead for all mankind of enlightenment and beneficial knowledge.

50

As religion inculcates morality, it is therefore the truest philosophy, and on it is built the only lasting civilization.

51

In all religions the belief exists that the soul survives the death of the body. Intercessions are sent up for the beloved dead, prayers are said for their progress and for the forgiveness of their sins.

52

It is because we have shut our eyes to the underlying principle of all religions, that God is one, that He is the Father of us all, that we are all immersed in the ocean of His mercy and sheltered and protected by His loving care. The glorious Sun of Truth shines for all alike, the waters of Divine Mercy immerse each one, and His Divine favor is bestowed on all His children.

53

It is evident that the fundamentals of religion are intended to unify and bind together; their purpose is universal, everlasting peace.

54

The day is coming when all the religions of the world will unite, for in principle they are one already. There is no need for division, seeing that it is only the outward forms that separate them. Among the sons of men some souls are suffering through ignorance, let us hasten to teach them; others are like children needing care and education until they are grown, and some are sick—to these we must carry Divine healing.

55

All down the ages we see how blood has stained the surface of the earth; but now a ray of greater light has come, man's intelligence is greater, spirituality is beginning to grow, and a time is surely coming when the religions of the world will be at peace. Let us leave the discordant arguments concerning outward forms, and let us join together to hasten forward the Divine Cause of unity, until all humanity knows itself to be one family, joined together in love.

56

Contemplate first the prejudice of religion: consider the nations of so-called religious people; if they were truly worshippers of God they would obey His law which forbids them to kill one another. If priests of religion really adored the God of love and served the Divine Light, they would teach their people to keep the chief Commandment, "To be in love and charity with all men." But we find the contrary, for it is often the priests who encourage nations to fight. Religious hatred is ever the most cruel! All religions teach that we should love one another; that we should seek out our own shortcomings before we presume to condemn the faults of others, that we must not consider ourselves superior to our neighbors! We must be careful not to exalt ourselves lest we be humiliated.

57

Man must cut himself free from all prejudice and from the result of his own imagination, so that he may be able to search for truth unhindered. Truth is one in all religions, and by means of it the unity of the world can be realized.

58

Religion should unite all hearts and cause wars and disputes to vanish from the face of the earth, give birth to spirituality, and bring life and light to each heart. If religion becomes a cause of dislike, hatred and division, it were better to be without it, and to withdraw from such a religion would be a truly religious act. For it is clear that the purpose of a remedy is to cure; but if the remedy should only aggravate the complaint it had better be left alone. Any religion which is not a cause of love and unity is no religion.

59

"Seek the truth, the truth shall make you free." So shall we see the truth in all religions, for truth is in all and truth is one!

60

I spoke yesterday of . . . "The Search for Truth"; how it is necessary for a man to put aside all in the nature of superstition, and every tradition which would blind his eyes to the existence of truth in all religions. He must not, while loving and clinging to one form of religion, permit himself to detest all others. It is essential that he search for truth in all religions, and, if his seeking be in earnest, he will assuredly succeed.

61

One Holy Soul gives life to the world of humanity, changes the aspect of the terrestrial globe, causes intelligence to progress, vivifies souls, lays the basis of a new life, establishes new foundations, organizes the world, brings nations and religions under the shadow of one standard, delivers man from the world of imperfections and vices, and inspires him with the desire and need of natural and acquired perfections.

62

Religion is the light of the world, and the progress, achievement, and happiness of man result from obedience to the laws set down in the holy Books.

63

Religion is a mighty stronghold . . . it must engender love, not malevolence and hate.

NOTES

From the Writings of Bahá'u'lláh

1. *Epistle to the Son of the Wolf,* p. 12.
2. *Gleanings from the Writings of Bahá'u'lláh,* no. 34.3.
3. Ibid., no. 34.5.
4. Ibid., no. 101.1.
5. *Tablets of Bahá'u'lláh,* pp. 63–64.
6. *Gleanings from the Writings of Bahá'u'lláh,* no. 27.5.
7. Ibid., no. 31.1.
8. Ibid., no. 22.3.
9. *Tablets of Bahá'u'lláh,* p. 159.
10. Ibid., p. 125.
11. Ibid., p. 129.
12. *Gleanings from the Writings of Bahá'u'lláh,* no. 34.3.

13. Ibid., no. 110.1.
14. Ibid., no. 84.3.
15. Ibid., no. 132.1.
16. Ibid., no. 24.1.
17. Ibid., no. 93.13.
18. Ibid., no. 162.2.
19. Kitáb-i-Íqán, ¶161.
20. *Gleanings from the Writings of Bahá'u'lláh*, no. 111.1.
21. Ibid., no. 93.15.
22. *Epistle to the Son of the Wolf,* p. 62.
23. *Gleanings from the Writings of Bahá'u'lláh*, no. 70.2.
24. Ibid., no. 34.7.
25. Ibid., no. 42.6.
26. *Prayers and Meditations,* p. 60.
27. *Summons of the Lord of Hosts,* no. 113.
28. *Tablets of Bahá'u'lláh,* p. 130.
29. Ibid., pp. 35–36.
30. *Gleanings from the Writings of Bahá'u'lláh*, no. 122.1.

31. *Tablets of Bahá'u'lláh,* p. 42.
32. Ibid., p. 91.
33. *Gleanings from the Writings of Bahá'u'lláh,* no. 22.3.
34. Ibid., no. 29.1

From the Writings of the Báb
1. *Selections from the Writings of the Báb,* no. 3:34:1.
2. Ibid., no. 2:51:1.
3. Ibid., no. 3:39:1.
4. Ibid., no. 3:31:1.
5. Ibid., no. 5:10:1.
6. Ibid., no. 4:9:3.
7. Ibid., no. 2:24:2.
8. Ibid., no. 3:15:3.

From the Writings of 'Abdu'l-Bahá
1. *Paris Talks,* no. 27.6.
2. *Selections from the Writings of 'Abdu'l-Bahá,* no. 227.21.
3. *Paris Talks,* no. 39.13.

4. *'Abdu'l-Bahá in London,* p. 28.

5. Ibid., p. 59.

6. *Selections from the Writings of 'Abdu'l-Bahá,* no. 23.6.

7. *'Abdu'l-Bahá in London,* p. 19.

8. *Promulgation of Universal Peace,* p. 175.

9. Ibid., p. 479.

10. Ibid., pp. 208–9.

11. Ibid., p. 551.

12. Ibid., p. 481.

13. Ibid., p. 446.

14. Ibid., p. 159.

15. Ibid., p. 213.

16. Ibid., p. 276.

17. *Selections from the Writings of 'Abdu'l-Bahá,* no. 17.4.

18. *Paris Talks,* no. 40.8.

19. *Promulgation of Universal Peace,* p. 118.

20. Ibid., p. 44.

21. Ibid., p. 134.

22. Ibid., p. 134.

23. *Selections from the Writings of 'Abdu'l-Bahá*, no. 102.1.
24. *Promulgation of Universal Peace*, p. 146.
25. *Selections from the Writings of 'Abdu'l-Bahá*, no. 13.1.
26. *Promulgation of Universal Peace*, p. 267.
27. Ibid., p. 56.
28. *'Abdu'l-Bahá in London*, p. 43.
29. *Selections from the Writings of 'Abdu'l-Bahá*, no. 23.2.
30. *Promulgation of Universal Peace*, p. 135.
31. *Paris Talks*, no. 13.16–13.17.
32. *Selections from the Writings of 'Abdu'l-Bahá*, no. 23.4.
33. Ibid., no. 34.5.
34. Ibid., no. 227.26.
35. *Promulgation of Universal Peace*, p. 58.
36. Ibid., p. 132.
37. Ibid., pp. 135–36.
38. Ibid., p. 137.
39. Ibid., p. 137.

40. Ibid., p. 138.

41. Ibid., p. 141.

42. Ibid., p. 162.

43. *Some Answered Questions,* p. 48.

44. *Promulgation of Universal Peace,* p. 169.

45. Ibid., p. 174.

46. Ibid., p. 175.

47. *'Abdu'l-Bahá in London,* p. 27.

48. *The Secret of Divine Civilization,* no. 135.

49. Ibid., no. 166.

50. *Paris Talks,* no. 7.4.

51. Ibid., no. 29.6.

52. Ibid., no. 39.7–39.8.

53. *Promulgation of Universal Peace,* p. 134.

54. *Paris Talks,* no. 39.15.

55. Ibid., no. 39.26.

56. Ibid., no. 45.4–45.6.

57. Ibid., no. 40.8.

58. Ibid., no. 40.14.

59. Ibid., no. 41.11.

60. Ibid., no. 42.1.

61. *Some Answered Questions*, p. 9.
62. *The Secret of Divine Civilization*, no. 130.
63. *Selections from the Writings of 'Abdu'l-Bahá*, no. 202.10.

BIBLIOGRAPHY

Works of Bahá'u'lláh

Epistle to the Son of the Wolf. New ed. Translated by
      Shoghi Effendi. 1st ps ed. Wilmette, IL:
      Bahá'í Publishing Trust, 1988.

Gleanings from the Writings of Bahá'u'lláh. Translated
      by Shoghi Effendi. Wilmette, IL: Bahá'í
      Publishing, 2005.

The Kitáb-i-Íqán: The Book of Certitude. Translated
      by Shoghi Effendi. Wilmette, IL: Bahá'í
      Publishing, 2003.

Prayers and Meditations. Translated by Shoghi Effendi.
      1st pocket-size ed. Wilmette, IL: Bahá'í Pub-
      lishing Trust, 1987.

The Summons of the Lord of Hosts: Tablets of Bahá'u'lláh.
      Wilmette, IL: Bahá'í Publishing, 2006.

Tablets of Bahá'u'lláh revealed after the Kitáb-i-Aqdas.
Compiled by the Research Department of
the Universal House of Justice. Translated
by Habib Taherzadeh et al. Wilmette, IL:
Bahá'í Publishing Trust, 1988.

Works of the Báb

Selections from the Writings of the Báb. Compiled by
the Research Department of the Universal
House of Justice. Translated by Habib Taherzadeh et al. Wilmette, IL: Bahá'í Publishing Trust, 2006.

Works of 'Abdu'l-Bahá

*'Abdu'l-Bahá in London: Addresses & Notes of Conver-
sations.* London: Bahá'í Publishing Trust, 1987.
*Paris Talks: Addresses Given By 'Abdu'l-Bahá in Paris in
1911.* Wilmette, IL: Bahá'í Publishing, 2006.
*Promulgation of Universal Peace: Talks Delivered by
'Abdu'l-Bahá during His Visit to the United
States and Canada in 1912.* Compiled by

Howard MacNutt. Wilmette, IL: Bahá'í
Publishing Trust, 2007.

The Secret of Divine Civilization. 1st pocket-size ed.
Translated by Marzieh Gail and Ali-Kuli
Khan. Wilmette, IL: Bahá'í Publishing, 2007.

Selections from the Writings of 'Abdu'l-Bahá. Compiled
by the Research Department of the Universal
House of Justice. Translated by a Committee
at the Bahá'í World Center and Marzieh
Gail. 1st pocket-size ed. Wilmette, IL: Bahá'í
Publishing, 2010.

Some Answered Questions. Compiled and translated
by Laura Clifford Barney. 1st pocket-size ed.
Wilmette, IL: Bahá'í Publishing Trust, 1984.

PUBLISHING

Bahá'í Publishing and the Bahá'í Faith

Bahá'í Publishing produces books based on the teachings of the Bahá'í Faith. Founded over 160 years ago, the Bahá'í Faith has spread to some 235 nations and territories and is now accepted by more than five million people. The word "Bahá'í" means "follower of Bahá'u'lláh." Bahá'u'lláh, the founder of the Bahá'í Faith, asserted that He is the Messenger of God for all of humanity in this day. The cornerstone of His teachings is the establishment of the spiritual unity of humankind, which will be achieved by personal transformation and the application of clearly identified spiritual principles. Bahá'ís also believe that there is but one religion and that all the Messengers of God—among them Abraham, Zoroaster, Moses, Krishna, Buddha, Jesus, and Muḥammad—have progressively revealed its nature. Together, the world's great religions are expressions of a single, unfolding divine plan. Human beings, not God's Messengers, are the source of religious divisions, prejudices, and hatreds.

The Bahá'í Faith is not a sect or denomination of another religion, nor is it a cult or a social movement. Rather, it is a globally recognized independent world religion founded on new books of scripture revealed by Bahá'u'lláh.

Bahá'í Publishing is an imprint of the National Spiritual Assembly of the Bahá'ís of the United States.

For more information about the Bahá'í Faith,
or to contact Bahá'ís near you,
visit http://www.bahai.us/
or call
1-800-22-UNITE

Other Books Available from
Bahá'í Publishing

COMPASSIONATE WOMAN
THE LIFE AND LEGACY OF PATRICIA LOCKE
John Kolstoe
$21.00 U.S. / $23.00 CAN
Hardcover
ISBN 978-1-931847-85-8

Compassionate Woman shares the captivating life of Patricia Locke, a Lakota Indian, who dedicated her life to righting injustices on behalf of indigenous peoples, as well as all of humanity. She was awarded the MacArthur Fellowship, was the first American Indian to serve as a senior officer on the National Spiritual Assembly of the Bahá'ís of the United States, and was posthumously inducted into the National Women's Hall of Fame.

This fascinating biography of Patricia Locke, who was given the name *Compassionate Woman*, gives us a glimpse into the life of someone dedicated to restoring justice and helping those in need. Her life of service began in Anchorage, Alaska, when she founded a community center aimed at assisting Native Americans, Eskimos, and Aleuts—who had moved to the city from villages—to cope with the many problems they encountered. She then went on to work for the Western Interstate Counsel for Higher Education, where she focused much of her energy on establishing colleges on Reservations. She was particularly concerned with improving education for American Indians, and worked hard toward advancing education on Reservations so that Native American culture and language could be woven into the curriculum. She also spent many years as a freelance writer, instructor at various universities, and activist on behalf of the poor and oppressed. In addition to the MacArthur Fellowship, Locke was the first American Indian to serve as a senior officer on the National Spiritual Assembly of the Bahá'ís of the United States, and was posthumously inducted into the National Women's Hall of Fame. Patricia Locke was wholeheartedly committed to serving the needs of others, and her indomitable spirit lives on through her legacy of service and loving compassion for all peoples of the world.

REJOICE IN MY GLADNESS

The Life of Ṭáhirih

Janet Ruhe-Schoen

$18.00 U.S. / $20.00 CAN

Trade Paper

ISBN 978-1-931847-84-1

A moving biography of one of the leading feminists of the 1800s, *Rejoice in My Gladness* traces the story of Ṭáhirih, a woman who began teaching the equality between men and women in largely Muslim Persia, and was eventually martyred for her outspokenness and courage.

Drawing on extensive research and steeped in the culture of daily life in nineteenth-century Persia, this is the definitive account of the life of Ṭáhirih—a renowned poetess and one of the leading feminists of her time. *Rejoice in My Gladness* follows the life of Ṭáhirih from her birth through her adulthood, covering important events such as her marriage, her controversial conversion to the Bábí Faith, and her execution due to her beliefs and activities. The reader will see how Ṭáhirih changed the face of women's rights forever, as she was the first woman in recorded Middle Eastern history to remove her veil before an assembly of men. At her execution, her last words have been recorded as "You can kill me as soon as you like, but you will never stop the emancipation of women."

THE QUICKENING

Unknown Poetry of Ṭáhirih
John S. Hatcher and Amrollah Hemmat
$18.00 U.S. / $20.00 CAN
Trade Paper
ISBN 978-1-931847-83-4

A new priceless collection of previously unpublished poems by the renowned nineteenth-century poetess, Ṭáhirih.

The Quickening is a newly translated collection of stirring poems by the renowned nineteenth-century poetess Ṭáhirih that deal with a subject that has challenged religious scholars throughout the ages. Among the world religions, no theme has attracted more attention or caused more controversy than the concept of a last judgment or end of time. The Bahá'í view of the "Resurrection," or the "Quickening," as the term is translated here, stands in bold contrast to many traditional views. It is seen as a prelude to a glorious outcome—the galvanizing of our collective will to bring about a just and lasting peace and the unification of humankind. In addition to the beautifully crafted English translation of Ṭáhirih's poems, this volume also includes her work in the original Persian and Arabic.

TALKS BY 'ABDU'L-BAHÁ

The Eternal Covenant

'Abdu'l-Bahá

$14.00 U.S. / $16.00 CAN

Hardcover

ISBN 978-1-931847-82-7

Spiritually uplifting and thought-provoking collection of talks from one of the central figures of the Bahá'í Faith.

Talks by 'Abdu'l-Bahá is a collection of talks given by 'Abdu'l-Bahá—the son and appointed successor of Bahá'u'lláh, the Prophet and Founder of the Bahá'í Faith—during his historic journey to North America in 1912. Speaking in front of diverse audiences, 'Abdu'l-Bahá offered profound insights on a number of topics in a simple manner accessible to anyone who listened with an open heart. The talks included in this volume all relate to the theme of the eternal covenant of God, one of the central themes of the teachings of the Bahá'í Faith. According to this covenant, God never leaves humankind alone without guidance but rather makes His will and purpose known to us through the appearance of His Prophets or Manifestations, Who appear periodically throughout history in order to advance human civilization.